THINK
LIKE A SELF-MADE
MILLIONAIRE

STEWART WELCH, III
America's Financial Advisor

WITH KAY RICE

NEW YORK

THINK LIKE A SELF-MADE MILLIONAIRE
10 Secrets to Success

© 2016 Stewart Welch III.

Published in New York, New York, by Morgan James Publishing. Morgan James and The Entrepreneurial Publisher are trademarks of Morgan James, LLC. www.MorganJamesPublishing.com

The Morgan James Speakers Group can bring authors to your live event. For more information or to book an event visit The Morgan James Speakers Group at www.TheMorganJamesSpeakersGroup.com.

Shelfie

A free eBook edition is available
with the purchase of this print book.

CLEARLY PRINT YOUR NAME ABOVE IN UPPER CASE

Instructions to claim your free eBook edition:
1. Download the Shelfie app for Android or iOS
2. Write your name in **UPPER CASE** above
3. Use the Shelfie app to submit a photo
4. Download your eBook to any device

ISBN 9781630476892 paperback
ISBN 9781630476908 eBook
ISBN 9781630476915 hardcover
Library of Congress Control Number: 2015910975

Cover and Interior Design by:
Chris Treccani
www.3dogdesign.net

In an effort to support local communities and raise awareness and funds, Morgan James Publishing donates a percentage of all book sales for the life of each book to Habitat for Humanity Peninsula and Greater Williamsburg.

Get involved today, visit
www.MorganJamesBuilds.com

Habitat for Humanity
Peninsula and
Greater Williamsburg
Building Partner

TABLE OF CONTENTS

ACKNOWLEDGEMENTS

Kay Rice has been a friend and encourager to me for more than a decade. Without her persistent nudging this book would have never been started, much less finished. Kay not only edited, but also provided valuable input related to content for this book. Thank you, Kay.

Harv Eker is the founder of Peak Potentials, one of the largest human development training companies in North America. I wanted to become a better public speaker and decided to attend seminars from three of the top speakers in the country. Harv was one of those three people. He is truly brilliant at designing courses that change people's lives and is just as brilliant on the stage. Harv gave me an opportunity to be an apprentice on his traveling training team and for about two years I crisscrossed America and Canada learning from the very best. Not only did I become a much better speaker,

Harv's concepts of human potential allowed me to grow as a person well beyond my expectations.

Doug Nelson. As an apprentice trainer at Peak Potentials, Doug was my trainer and mentor. Doug is a great teacher both on stage and off. Just as important, he and his beautiful wife, Melanie, are two of the finest people I know. I learned a lot just being around them!

Jack Canfield. I spent the better part of a week with a small group of folks at Jack Canfield's vacation home in Hawaii. Jack is a gentle giant of a man whose thoughtful insights had a great influence on me and everyone in the group. Jack is the master of processes that guide you to expand your world, or become a bigger you, so that you can, in turn, help others.

Stewart Welch, Jr. At age 97, my father still manages to inspire me! He still drives, lives alone, keeps his own (big) yard and comes into work every day. He's still actively thinking of new financial strategies to help people save money, avoid estate taxes and save the country!

Maryann Brown, CreativeMarketingCafe.com put in many hours to help with the branding and design for Get Rich On Purpose® from the original cover design concept for the book series to our online branding for our website and social media. Thank you, Maryann.

INTRODUCTION

Here's my story (and I'm sticking to it!):

In my early adolescent years, I was what I call a "cruiser"—someone who cruised through life doing just enough to stay under my parent's radar. I cruised through high school in the middle of the pack; then cruised into college, the one that was easiest for me to get into; then cruised into the easiest major at the time: marketing. As I graduated, I cruised into my first job—life insurance sales (if you could fog a mirror, you were hired!). But about six months after I started working, something happened. It was like a lightning bolt hit me. I made a *decision* that I would become a millionaire by age forty! Now, a million dollars is a lot of money today, but back in the seventies, it was the equivalent of climbing Mt.

Everest! I had no clue how I would accomplish this feat—I thought and thought, and then I hatched "The Plan." The best way to become a millionaire, I thought to myself, was to *study* Self-Made Millionaires, then *model* their behavior. In other words, I would get inside their minds and then do what they did.

So you may ask, at the age of 22, how did I find and model Self-Made Millionaires? Granted, my peers were not millionaires. I looked for models and mentors through books. I paid attention to those around me who had become successful, and I even hosted a TV show, *Welch Profiles: Personal Success Stories*, where I interviewed Self-Made Millionaires. My bottom line? Find and interview (ask questions of) as many Self-Made Millionaires as possible. I found most were open to sharing their wisdom. All you had to do was ask! Over a few short years, what emerged was the realization that these extraordinarily successful people all shared a handful of characteristics, or what I refer to as their "Secrets to Success," that set them apart from everyone else. These success characteristics transformed ordinary people into multi-millionaires who achieved extraordinary results. I modeled and applied these success secrets in my own life, and guess what? My strategy worked! By applying what I learned, I achieved my goal of becoming a Self-Made Millionaire before the age of 40. With immaturity and lack of experience came lots of mistakes, and I now realize that if I had known then what I know now, I could have become a millionaire much sooner. For one thing, most people naturally possess some of the characteristics of Self-Made Millionaires. However, if you are missing just one or two of the 10 Secrets to Success described in this book, your chances of becoming a millionaire are very low. Yep. It takes knowing and implementing all 10!

Who would you say is the wealthiest person you know personally? How did he or she achieve their wealth? Is it possible for you to achieve similar wealth? Yes! It is as possible as you think it is! Most of the wealthy people I know built their fortunes themselves. This is the definition of self-made wealth: it is not inherited, acquired through marriage, or won in the lottery. It's built with hard work, determination and passion.

What is the definition of wealth? Webster's dictionary defines wealth as an "abundance of valuable material possessions or resources," and the word wealthy is defined as "extremely affluent." The definition of affluent sounds even better: "having a generously sufficient and typically increasing supply of material possessions." Well then, what is Financial Freedom, and how does it fit in? Financial Freedom means you have sufficient *passive income* to pay for your lifestyle. Passive income is income from sources not dependent on your showing up and having to work at a job from 9 to 5 every day. Passive income sources might include things like income from investments, cash flow positive real estate and business interests. I know our goal is that we would all like to be Financially Free, at least by the time we retire. Unfortunately, statistics show that only about 5% of our population ever reaches that goal. Every single person I have ever met who has achieved Financial Freedom has what I call the right *mindset* for success. They have the right mindset and the right characteristics, and have used the secrets I describe in this book. What I want you to know is that it is not that hard to become rich. It's just a matter of doing the right things in the right order, and doing them consistently.

If you are reading this, then you likely are interested in becoming rich. Most everyone we know would like to be rich, although not everyone is willing to admit it. There is so much negative connotation with the word *rich*, I'm going to change the vocabulary and use the words *Financial Freedom*. Who could object to being Financially Free?

So why do so few people actually become Financially Free? What do people do to become Financially Free? Why can't everyone do it? The fact is that anyone can!

Do you have what it takes to be Financially Free?

Anyone can become rich, or Financially Free, if they have the right characteristics and implement the right habits. I've designed a short quiz to help you determine if you have what it takes to become Financially Free. This quiz is based solely on the experiences of wealthy people I have met, almost all of whom share certain habits and characteristics. The results will suggest whether becoming Financially Free will be relatively easy for you or a bit more of a challenge. Take a moment to complete the quiz right now:

The Wealth Quiz

Answer each question below "Yes" or "No" and keep count of how many "Yes" and "No" answers you have.

1. Do you enjoy your work?

2. Do you often visualize yourself achieving something bigger than what you are currently doing?

3. Do you save money every month?

4. Do you invest at least some of your money directly in the stock market either through a 401(k), individual stocks, or mutual funds?

5. Do you shop before you buy most of the time, especially for big-ticket items?

6. Do you take care of your home or apartment, performing regular maintenance as well as repairs?

7. Do you perform regular maintenance on your car and other expensive items?

8. Do you pay off the full balance on your credit cards each month?

9. Are you comfortable buying used big-ticket items such as cars and appliances?

10. Have you ever started your own business (even a lemonade stand counts)?

11. Have you ever estimated how much money you would need in an investment portfolio to produce enough income to cover your current living expenses?

12. Do you measure the performance results of your portfolio at least yearly?

13. Do you maximize your personal contribution to your IRA or company's 401(k) plan?

14. Is your mortgage payment less than 20 percent of your total gross household income? OR, if you do not own a home, is your rent less than 20 percent of your total gross household income?

15. Do you spend less than you make?

16. Have you ever read a book about building wealth or an autobiography about someone who was wealthy?

17. Do you have your own business now that produces a positive net income?

18. Have you ever worked all night or more than 24 hours on a project?

For each question that you answered yes, give yourself one point.

Total these points and then compare the total to the scale below to check the probability of becoming wealthy.

Score	Probability of Becoming Rich
1–5	Low
6 –10	Average

| 11–15 | Very likely |
| 16–18 | You are on your way! |

Well, how did you do?

If you scored poorly, don't worry. It just means that you'll need to focus some attention on the mental side of the money game; replace old thought patterns and habits with new ones that support success. We'll talk about how to do that later in the book. If you scored well, congratulations! A few tweaks to what you're doing and you'll be well on your way to Financial Freedom! For all of you, your score just identifies both your strong and weak points. Take a moment and look at the questions to which you answered "No" and think about what changes you could make to turn each "No" into a "Yes." The bottom line is that anyone can become Financially Free and I'm going to show you how!

I developed the *Get Rich On Purpose® book series* and website with a single goal in mind. With my remaining time on Earth, I want to help as many people as I possibly can by showing them how to achieve sustainable Financial Freedom. Are you ready to learn what it will take to become Financially Free?

A few parting thoughts…

So, what do people *really* want regarding their personal finances?

Everyone at least wants to be Financially Free, if not wealthy. For if you are not Financially Free, it means that you are *dependent* upon someone else for your basic support. And no adult wants that. So, if everyone wants it, why is it that so few ever achieve it? Most of the answers can be found in what you have learned about money up until now, as well as the money habits you have formed. And, in reality, most of you will need to unlearn much of what you think you know about money *and* adopt new money habits. You will need to create the right mindset in order to become Financially Free. This book is designed to help you do just that.

The least you need to know

- Wealth can be built by anyone at any age if they are willing to learn and develop the necessary habits and characteristics of Self-Made Millionaires. Start identifying the common misconceptions about wealth, and don't let them hold you back from achieving your fortune.

- To build real wealth, you have to believe that it can be done.

- Wealth is a journey that requires a high level of tenacity and determination to overcome the occasional setbacks.

- To profit most from this book, complete the Opportunity Assignments at the end of each chapter.

Chapter 1

The Secret of Decision

"The indispensable first step to getting what you want out of life is this: Decide what you want."

—Ben Stein

If you are reading this book, then it is probably safe to say that you want more money in your life. Most people say they would like to accumulate wealth and become Financially Free. However, wishing for money and wealth is not good enough. I am about to share with you what is perhaps the most important of the 10 Secrets to Success. Here it is: In order to become Financially Free, you must make a *passionate decision* to become Financially Free.

Unfortunately, most people are so busy living their lives that they don't stop to think about what they truly want. Oh sure, they have passing thoughts: "I wish I had more money," "I wish I were rich," "I wish I didn't have so many bills," "I wish my spouse/children didn't spend so much money," "I wish my parents were rich so I could inherit a fortune." I'm sure you have a few that you could add to this list. However, there's no substance to these thoughts—and in fact, at best, they are nothing more than idle daydreams.

So what is the difference between wishing for more money in your life and making a *passionate*, destiny-altering *decis*ion to become Financially Free? In this chapter I am going to walk you through what it will take to *decide* to become Financially Free and show you how to give power to your decision. Today may turn out to be the most important day in your financial life. Remember, everything created in the material universe began with a thought and a desire. Your thoughts, desires and actions are what create your reality. Make no mistake: our thoughts are things and they are very powerful, more powerful than you may realize. In this way, your thoughts, decisions and actions today will create your reality tomorrow. Where you are today is the result of the thoughts, decisions and actions you have taken up until this point.

Take a moment and reflect back on the time since your first job. All of the financial decisions that you have made up until this time have gotten you where you are today, financially speaking. If you are perfectly happy with those decisions and with your current financial circumstances, then congratulations! Keep doing what has been successful for you. I hope that you'll stick with THINK *Like a Self-Made Millionaire* because I believe you'll pick up some gems that can accelerate your speed of success.

STEWART H WELCH III

For those of you who are not satisfied with your results, congratulations! You have just found the key to unlocking the driver, or the passion it will take to make the kind of decision that will change your life forever! Every decision you make, every desire you have, is based on either seeking pleasure or avoiding pain. More often the most passionate decisions, the ones that have the most power, are based on avoiding pain. This is the point where the pain is so great that you'll do just about anything to change your situation. I want you to *know* that you have the power to change. And yes, there's still plenty of time.

I'm reminded of an old movie starring Peter Finch and Faye Dunaway called *Network*. In the movie, Peter plays a network TV anchor who finally goes berserk after reporting one bad news story after another and screams on air, "I'm mad as hell, and I'm not going to take it anymore!" His mantra catches on and everyone is opening their windows, sticking their heads out and screaming as well. My question to you is: Have you had enough yet? If you have, then it's

decision that you're NOT going to take it

sion is, starting today, to do whatever it

Become Financially Free! If you make that decision, I will help you. If you don't make that decision, then you are doomed to a future built upon the past. The decision is yours. Choose wisely!

Once you have made a *passionate decision* to take control of your financial future, you will have what it takes to be totally committed to your decision. The *passion* and *commitment* are what give your decision the *power* to bring it into reality. This is no longer a "maybe I'll try" type of decision, but rather an *"I'll do whatever it takes!"* commitment to your decision about your financial success. Total commitment to your decision is an attitude of the will.

In my experience over the past thirty-plus years, few people are willing to make this level of commitment to their financial success. In fact, research suggests that 95% of people never achieve financial independence. So what's going to make it different for you? What level of *commitment* will be requ

for you to be accepted into the most private of clubs—**Th**

5% Club—the 5% of the population who *do* achieve financial

independence? You must have an unrelenting laser focus

on a predetermined destination. In other words, you must

decide exactly what you want, and then never take your eye

off the prize until you have it!

Here's a history lesson that illuminates the total commitment

and passion which gives a decision the power to bring it into

reality:

The Mongolian warriors were known as the fiercest warriors in

history. The reason? They believed in total commitment to their

cause. How did they express their commitment? They would

pack all of their family, wives and children, and all of their

possessions on their boats and sail to the land they intended

to conquer. Upon arrival, they'd unload everything and set up

camp on the shores. Then they'd burn their boats! You see, for

them, defeat was not an option. If they lost the battle, if they lost the war, they would lose not only their lives and all of their possessions, but their wives and children would become slaves.

What achievement would you be willing to be totally committed to?

You've heard people say, "Be careful what you commit to." This is because a commitment is a promise that you've made. If you break promises that you make to other people, they will quickly learn that you cannot be trusted, and trust is one of the most important character traits one can possess. Break promises to yourself, and you'll lose both faith and confidence in yourself. The good news is that you can build trust by keeping your commitments to others and yourself. Are you ready to plant the seed of total commitment to becoming Financially Free? If so, I would be pleased to travel with you on your journey. It will be fun, challenging at times, and easier than you think.

Opportunity Assignment

Are you ready for me to walk you through a process to bring your decision to become Financially Free into a reality? Are you ready to become totally committed?

DECISION STEPS

1. The first step in the process is to decide what you want and then write it down! I'm not sure how to explain it, but something magical happens when you articulate your true desires on paper. A connection is made between you and the Universe and your chances of success are magnified many-fold. Make it measurable. Decide on the exact amount of money you wish to accumulate and the date by which you intend to have it.

2. The second step is to determine exactly what kind of service you intend to give to the world in return for this sum of money. Money is energy, and serves

---

as a measuring stick of the service you give to the world. I believe we all came to this earth with certain talents to share. You will generally find those talents in things that you are passionate about or enjoy the most!

3. Next, you must fuel your decision with passion and commitment by building a compelling *why*. Write down why being Financially Free is important to you. Look for the compelling *why's* like, "So I can send my children to the best schools," or "So I have the time and resources to help needy children." If you can get the *why* right, the *how* will become much easier.

4. Finally, once you've written it down (and here's the scary part), share it with someone. Hopefully that someone is a person who's in a position to support you and your progress, like a spouse, significant other or close friend.

An unconditional commitment that you make to yourself—one that you commit to writing, one that you share with someone you care about and who cares about you—now that *is* something different. I suspect you can *feel* the difference. Is that true for you?

ACTION STEP: Use the My Commitment form at the end of this section to write down the financial goal you are committed to achieving. Don't wait. Do this NOW!

Nice job! Go ahead, pat yourself on the back! Now that you've put your commitment in writing, go back and re-read it. You should feel some strong emotions: passion; a sense of importance or urgency; a sense of determination; or a sense of empowerment. If not, re-think what it is that you truly want for your personal finances.

As additional support....

form for you   a commitment where you'll

o yourself in   t you place it somewhere

uitment form   your statement to yourself

py with you,

If you would

going to the   commitment with someone.

com, where   n you value and who cares

                      accountability partner and

                      iew your progress towards

you've never gone,
ou've never done…

unknown

ice of success:
d an unremitting devotion
want to see happen.

loyd Wright

To help you, we've created a My Commitmen

to fill in to help you put your commitment

writing. You will find a copy of the My Com:

on the following page. Fill it out and carry a c

and post a copy where you will see it every day

like to print a copy of this form, you can do so b

Resource section of www.GetRichOnPurpos

you will find a downloadable copy.

MY COMMITMENT

I, _____ (*your name*), am totally committed to my financial future and achieving Financial Freedom. I will accumulate at least $_____ dollars by _____, 20 __ and/or will have an income of at least $_____ per _____ (*year/ month/week*), and a passive income of not less than $ _____ per _____ (*year/month/week*).

In return for this amount of money I will offer the following talents or services to the world: _____

_____

_____.

I am passionate about my commitment because: (*make sure you have a big enough* why!) _____

_____

_____

_____.

My thoughts from this chapter…

_____

_____

_____

_____

_____

_____

_____

You'll want to keep your written commitment where you'll see it often, so I recommend that you place it somewhere where you will see it daily. Read your statement to yourself at least twice each day.

Finally, I want you to share your commitment with someone. Choose someone whose opinion you value and who cares about you. Ask them to be your accountability partner and agree to meet regularly to review your progress towards achieving your goal(s).

In order to go where you've never gone,
you must do what you've never done...

—Author unknown

I know the price of success:
dedication, hard work, and an unremitting devotion
to the things you want to see happen.

—Frank Lloyd Wright

To help you, we've created a My Commitment form for you to fill in to help you put your commitment to yourself in writing. You will find a copy of the My Commitment form on the following page. Fill it out and carry a copy with you, and post a copy where you will see it every day. If you would like to print a copy of this form, you can do so by going to the Resource section of www.GetRichOnPurpose.com, where you will find a downloadable copy.

THINK LIKE A SELF-MADE MILLIONAIRE

down this book or turn off the computer and go catch the latest re-run of *The Big Bang Theory*! However, if it's your dream to discover just what your true potential is, then you are in the right place!

To emphasize the importance of *clarity* in achieving the outcome you want, imagine this. You decide you would like to have a new car. So you send a message out into the Universe that you want a new car, and guess what? Very soon, you get a new car! It is a 1965 Mustang convertible! This is a cute car. It is a classic and it is new to you, but maybe it isn't exactly what you had in mind. You forgot to tell the Universe what kind of new car you wanted! So let's improve the clarity in your vision about what kind of new car you really want. Now let's suppose you decide you want a new or pre-owned BMW, Mercedes, or Lexus. You can't decide, but you just know that you want a nice luxury car. Your indecision and lack of clarity is still a little fuzzy here. You are still not sending a clear message out about what you want. Therefore you will be less certain about what you will get and when. I've learned that fuzzy intentions give me fuzzy results. So let's get even more clarity. What do you really want? OK, we're getting closer. So finally you have decided that you want a black, 2015, pre-owned 645i BMW with tan leather seats and less than 50,000 miles on it. Now let's look in the paper or go to the local BMW dealership and test drive one! Now you have absolute clarity and you've sent a very clear message about what you want out into the Universe. By actually test driving the car, you have a very clear vision of what it will be like, and what it will look, feel, and even smell like to have the car you desire. This is clarity!

In studying Self-Made Millionaires for the past 30 years, I discovered that much of their success could be attributed to their clarity about their intended result. They knew what they want to achieve even if they did not know how they were going to achieve it. This vision becomes a fixation that evokes energy, passion and enthusiasm and is a primary driver of daily thoughts—and ultimately actions. Of course the danger is that the vision becomes a fixation to the exclusion of all else. We all know someone (someone sitting in your chair right now, maybe?) who is a workaholic. Well, don't use this fixation as an excuse not to play, because I'll show you how to make sure you create a nice balance in your life in a later chapter.

TIP: There's nothing wrong with short bursts of workaholic-mode—in fact, it can be quite stimulating, and productive and release your innate creativity. Get stuck in workaholic-mode and you'll eventually reach burn-out—definitely not good!

Have you ever noticed how some people seem to have extraordinary luck? Well, I've heard more than one wise person describe luck as being nothing more than opportunity meeting preparedness. And one of the best ways to prepare yourself for the arrival of the opportunities and circumstances to help you achieve your goals is through clarity, or having a clear vision of the outcome that you desire. Once you have impressed a clear vision upon your mind, you have, in effect,

19

sent a message out into the Universe. You have called into motion forces beyond our comprehension which begin to orchestrate circumstances and events to fulfill your desires. You will notice that things begin to happen to support the outcome you desire. And when you expect things to show up, you open yourself up to the opportunities that will appear. On the level of quantum physics, this has to do with resonance. Remember, thoughts have power. Therefore, when you send a very clear thought or a vibration out into the Universe, it tends to attract other thoughts and vibrations which match up with it. You actually begin to become a magnet that attracts opportunities and situations that will help you achieve your desires. Some people call this luck, others call this coincidence, and some people seem to have mastered this.

How about a story to illustrate this?

This man was a little-known comedian in 1990 who clearly envisioned himself as a top-paid Hollywood movie star. To help maintain focus on his vision, he wrote a check payable to himself for $10 million—"for acting services rendered," and dated the check Thanksgiving 1995. He worked hard at his craft and kept the check in his wallet so that every time he opened it, he was reminded of his vision, his goal, his intention. His big break came in 1994 when he starred in three films: *Ace Ventura, Pet Detective; The Mask;* and *Dumb and Dumber.* By 1995, Jim Carey was one of Hollywood's highest paid actors at $20 million per film.

In order to create clarity around your vision of Financial Freedom, I want you to take a few moments to imagine what that will be like. I want you to imagine it on every level. What kind of house will you own, and where will it be located? What will your life be like on a day-to-day basis? What will it feel like to do, be and have the freedom each day to do exactly what you want, when you want, and with whom you want? Make it as real as you possibly can by imagining with all five of your senses what your life will be like when you have accomplished what you want.

I'm reminded of scholar, philosopher, and researcher of Human Capacities Jean Houston describing her dear friend, Margaret Mead, and her ability to manifest her desires into reality through her powerful process of visualizing what she wanted. She would run the scenario through her mind imagining what the emerging future would be like with images, feelings, touch and taste. She visualized her desired outcome using not only feelings, facts, and images, but she would use all five of her senses: smell, taste, sight, touch and sound. She would create her own movie of what her future would be like if she took various actions, and then she would refine it further, playing out a variety of outcomes and deciding on which actions would create the vision and the reality with the most positive outcome. In this way, she became a walking magnet of the reality and the outcomes she wanted to create.

I have personally experienced the power of creating a clear vision in my own life so many times I have lost count. In 1996, I set an intention and created a vision of having a personal finance book published by "a big, fancy, white-shoe publisher in New York." Certainly, none of my English teachers would have believed this possible! I did not have a natural ability or affinity for writing, but I knew a published book would be one of the best methods to get my message out to tens of thousands of people—and that was my vision. Well, intention became reality with my first publishing contract with Simon & Schuster in 1998. Since then, I have had three additional books published by three different "big, fancy, white-shoe New York publishing firms," including the book that inspired this book, *The Complete Idiot's Guide to Getting Rich* (Alpha, a member of Penguin Group publishers).

I wrote an article called **"Turning Dreams into Reality,"** which describes a powerful visioning process. Read the article (which you can find at the back of this book), and then fill out the vision worksheet that I created. You will find a copy of the vision worksheet at the end of this chapter. You can also find a downloadable copy of the worksheet under the Resource section at **www.GetRichOnPurpose.com**.

This leads me to the Universal Law of Intention—

The Universal Law of Intention states that by the mere fact of you creating a clear intention, the Universe will set in motion forces needed to make your intention become a reality. True, you have to be alert to the opportunities the Universe sends you and act on those opportunities, but the results will show up in your life if you'll allow them.

On a personal level, I believe that God created the Universe and everything in it, so everything and everybody is connected. All of the answers to all of your questions are available to you if you know where to go or whom to ask.

For example, when I set the intention to have a book published, I had no idea how to make that happen. I just trusted the Universe. One day I got a call from a lady who had been a writer for *Money* magazine and had interviewed me as a financial expert on several occasions for articles she was writing. She had recently moved to a publishing house owned by Simon & Schuster and wanted to know if I'd be interested in submitting a proposal to author a book titled, *10 Minute Guide to Personal Finances for Newlyweds*. Having set the intention to write a book, I naturally jumped at the chance. I then went into workaholic-mode, and in a couple of days, delivered a very professional and detailed proposal (the speed of delivering the proposal and the professional detail of the proposal impressed the publisher). They accepted, and (knees knocking!) I set about writing the book. Was I scared? YES! Was I worried that in having no writing experience (zilch, nada, none) I might fail? YES! But again, I trusted in the Universe and intuitively knew that I would do whatever it took to succeed. I did succeed, and this became my first book published by a big, fancy, New York publisher!

So, if you were Financially Free, how would you know? What exactly does Financial Freedom mean to you? Let me help you out here with my definition. *You are Financially Free at that point in time when you have passive income equal to or greater than the income needed to pay for your desired lifestyle.* The key word here is *passive*. This means that you have cash flow coming in automatically without having to work for it—.i.e. you have the *choice* of working or not working.

You may want to use a different definition. Some people will use a specific dollar amount such as $5 million. What's important is that it is *your* definition AND that it be measurable by someone else. In other words, if you share your definition with me, I'd know when you achieved it. Make sense? Now it's your turn.

Opportunity Assignment

1. Review your Commitment form (Chapter 1) and see how you could rewrite your Commitment so that it more clearly expresses what success looks like for you. You need to be specific enough so that anyone else reading it would be able to tell when you've achieved it. In other words, it needs to be *measurable*.

2. Share your revised Financial Freedom definition with someone (are you beginning to get the concept of the power, or leverage, of having an accountability partner?).

3. If you haven't already done so, read about the visioning process in my article, "Turning Dreams into Reality" and fill out the Vision worksheet. You can find a copy of the article at the back of this book. The Vision worksheet is on the next page. A downloadable copy of the worksheet can be found at **GetRichOnPurpose.com** under the Resource tab.

My Vision:

Compelling WHY:

I: Critical Success Factor:

    Supporting Action:

    Supporting Action:

    Supporting Action:

II: Critical Success Factor:

    Supporting Action:

    Supporting Action:

    Supporting Action:

III: Critical Success Factor:

    Supporting Action:

    Supporting Action:

    Supporting Action:

My thoughts from this chapter…

_____

_____

_____

_____

_____

_____

_____

Chapter 3

The Secret of Belief

*"Whether you think you can or you can't...
you're right."*

—Henry Ford

In order to change your reality, you must change your thoughts. When you change your thoughts you change your beliefs, and when you change your beliefs you change your reality. Have you witnessed someone who has been held back from achieving a goal in life because of their own self-limiting beliefs? Have you ever seen someone who just did not believe something good could actually happen to them? Maybe someone who didn't believe they could actually be successful? Have you ever known a person who believes that his or her lot in life is to be bound by poverty and failure? Your beliefs, whether they are good or bad, whether you believe in success or failure, create a self-fulfilling prophecy.

Please take a moment and examine your own beliefs. Do you believe you are capable of achieving the success and the Financial Freedom you desire? Do you believe you are 'worthy' of success? Some people have been raised with or have acquired self-limiting beliefs which will hold them back. The great news is that we can change our beliefs. Our subconscious mind is like a computer. Have you ever heard the expression, "garbage in, garbage out?" Well, if we have filled our subconscious mind with self-limiting beliefs, then our results will also be limited. The wonderful news is that our subconscious mind will "believe" whatever you tell it. Therefore, there is nothing to hinder you from re-programming your subconscious mind with a new set of beliefs that support your goals.

*"I do not allow my mind to think a thought
without my permission."*

—Rama Berch

Once you have identified any self-limiting beliefs, you can replace them with a better thought or suggestion. Some people may consider this deceiving our subconscious mind, but the truth is our minds do not evaluate the thoughts and beliefs with which we program it. It just begins to orchestrate situations and events to "match up" our beliefs and our thoughts with our reality. Therefore, in order to re-program your subconscious, conduct yourself and your thoughts "as if" you already have the thing that you desire. Maybe you've heard the saying, "fake it until you make it."

I once suggested this to a group of people, and someone piped up and asked, "So if you want to become a multi-millionaire, does this mean you go out and start spending money?" Let's think about this. Do you really believe a habit of a Self-Made Millionaire is to spend money they don't already have? My suggestion was that perhaps you could ask a better question, such as "How can I manage my money in a way that a Millionaire manages his or her money? How can I think and behave "as if" I've already achieved Financial Freedom? What thoughts and habits do Millionaires use to attract money and money-making opportunities to them?" I believe you will find that Self-Made Millionaires spend less time on spending money and more time on making money! You can begin thinking and behaving as a Millionaire and state to yourself that you already are a Millionaire who is just waiting for your money to be deposited into your bank account! Begin to think like a millionaire; learn what millionaires think about and how they invest their money; visualize your life as a millionaire; and begin to do the things they do. Eventually you, too, will become a millionaire. If you don't believe it, you will not achieve it! We are all worthy of Financial Freedom and achieving wealth, but in order to receive it, you must believe it is possible for *you*.

*"You have a divine right to abundance;
and if you are anything less than a millionaire, you
haven't had your fair share."*

—Stuart Wilde

If you have any doubts about your worthiness of achieving wealth, tape that quote on your bathroom mirror and repeat it to yourself every day when you get up and brush your teeth, and again at night before you go to bed.

The *Law of Belief* is well stated in the following popular verse that I have seen in many Athletic Departments and coaches' offices:

*"If you think you are beaten you are,
If you think you dare not, you don't
If you like to win, but you think you can't
It is almost certain you won't.*

*If you think you'll lose you're lost
For out of the world we find
Success begins with a fellow's will —
It's all in the state of mind.*

*If you think you are outclassed you are,
You've got to think high to rise,
You've got to be sure of yourself before
You can ever win a prize.*

Life's battles don't always go
To the stronger or faster man,
But soon or later the man who wins…

Is the man WHO THINKS HE CAN!"

—Walter D. Wintle

I believe that God does not allow us to conceive any worthy goal without the ability to achieve it. This means that within every desire we have, so long as it is in line with service and the other natural laws of the Universe, there are the mechanics and the ability to fulfill that desire. Therefore, I encourage you to Dream Big Dreams! Believe you can accomplish your goals and desires and live your life fully in the direction of achieving those dreams. If you set your goals on something small, if you already know exactly how you will fulfill your goals, chances are your dream isn't big enough! I encourage you to dream a dream that is big enough that without the wisdom of the Universe, without a few 'coincidences' and unexpected 'opportunities' showing up, you would not know exactly how you would fulfill that dream. Then believe it is possible and begin to "expect" things to show up to support your vision.

Many people stop just short of their dreams, so NEVER GIVE UP! Stay focused on the outcome you want, and continue to take actions that move you towards your dream until it has become manifest in your life. This is the secret of all great masters—they keep moving forward, staying persistent, focused and single-minded about the thing until they have created it in reality.

A Personal Example

An example in my own life was my dream of becoming a Black Belt in Karate. I've never been a gifted athlete so excelling at anything physical always required a lot of work. I remember when I first met my instructor, Master Chung, a tenth degree black belt from South Korea who spoke only broken English. I told him I may not be his best (most gifted) student, but I would be one of his hardest working—and his favorite! Well, I did work hard, and it took me quite a long time before he finally granted me the opportunity to test for my black belt. Frankly, I think he allowed me to test out of pity! As part of the test, we had to perform six double-board breaks and one concrete break. Fail any of the breaks, and you fail the test. Breaking one board is, well, not too difficult. But when you put two together, you have to have both power and technique to get the job done. My concrete break was a downward punch where I broke the concrete (on my second try) and split my knuckle! I did a hammer heel double board strike where I severely bruised my heel. I did a hammer fist strike, a forearm strike, a side kick, a roundhouse kick, and was basically out of working body parts. One to go—no body parts uninjured. Then I thought, "I could try to do my last break with a double board shin strike." I had never tried this, and he had never taught it, so when I announced my next break, Master Chung came running over and said, "No, that is too dangerous!"

I asked if he would pass me with only five board breaks and he said, "No."

I said, "Then I'm going to do it!"

I did the break and my shin immediately swelled to about twice its normal size!

The point is that I believed I could meet the challenge. Even though I was not certain of success, I was certain that success would elude me if I didn't try. To succeed, you must get comfortable moving outside of your comfort zone. Staying in your comfort zone will keep you exactly where you are now.

I'll conclude by this powerful quote from Marianne Williamson, which was used by Nelson Mandela in his 1994 inaugural speech.

"Our deepest fear is not that we are inadequate. Our deepest fear is that we are powerful beyond measure. It is our light, not our

darkness that frightens us most. We ask ourselves, 'Who am I to be brilliant, gorgeous, talented, and famous?' Actually, who are you NOT to be? You are a child of God. You playing small does not serve the world. There is nothing enlightened about shrinking so that people won't feel insecure around you. We were born to make manifest the glory of God that is within us. It's not just in some of us; it's in all of us. And when we let our own light shine, we unconsciously give other people permission to do the same. As we are liberated from our own fear, our presence automatically liberates others."

Opportunity Assignment

Make a list of all of the things you would like to do, be or have. I call this my Dream Big Dreams™ list. To access a downloadable copy of my Dream Big Dreams list, visit 'Resources' at **www.GetRichOnPurpose.com.** Dream Big! Your goal is to have your list exceed 100 entries. What I have found is that most people begin their list with 'stuff' they want: a nice home, car, furnishings, large bank account, and great vacations. With the goal being 100 entries, they begin to run out of 'stuff' ideas and begin to reach out into how they can help others, such as giving to a charity or going on an extended mission trip. It's in this area that many people begin to recognize their purpose in life, their true passion, their God-given talent. For me, this exercise helped me realize that I have a gift, a passion, and desire to help as many people as possible achieve their greatest financial potential.

Yep. In many cases, we have to get at least some of the 'stuff' of life out of the way before we are ready to really reach out and help others in a significant way.

Keep your list in a safe place and from time to time pull it out and check off the things as they have been fulfilled or accomplished.

My thoughts from this chapter…

_____

_____

_____

_____

_____

_____

_____

Chapter 4

The Secret of Decisive Action

"Stop thinking, start doing—it will give you power!"
—Stewart Welch III

Anybody can wish for riches, and most people do, but only a few know that following a plan of *decisive action* plus making a *clear and passionate decision* to become Financially Free are the only dependable means of accumulating wealth.

It doesn't matter who you are, what you do, or what your current situation is, you have the power to change. One of the key characteristics of Self-Made Millionaires is that they get into 'Action' both early and often. You've heard the mantra, "ready, aim, fire!" Well, a Self-Made Millionaire's mantra is, "READY, *FIRE*, AIM!" They decide the result they want to achieve, such as becoming Financially Free, then they gather as much information as they can in a short period of time, then they take *action*, often not knowing if the action they have chosen is the best choice among many choices. They figure the best way to 'learn the game' is to be *'in'* the game. And, in my experience, it's true. The best way to learn anything is to do it, and then make changes as needed. If you find something that doesn't work, *change your course of action*. When you find something that does work, do more of it. Once you are in the game, the mantra becomes, **"CORRECT AND CONTINUE!"**

Take investing for example. To become Financially Free, you will almost certainly need to learn how to invest. So what's the best way to learn? Read some books? Take a course or seminar? Talk to professional investors? All of these are good ideas and will increase your knowledge. But the single best strategy for learning how to invest is to (drum roll here) actually invest! There's nothing like having a little 'skin' in the game to focus your attention. If you would like to learn more about investing, check out *How to Become a Smart Investor* in our Get Rich on Purpose® book series.

How I got my financial start

I applied this principle at age 22, starting with a very small amount of money, 10% of my rather modest paycheck, being automatically transferred into a savings account. At first it seemed inconsequential and a waste of time. But over a number of months, the account balance began to take on more meaning. I also found this little bit of success encouraged me to save more. It became almost a game. I liked seeing my account get bigger and bigger! A few years later, the owner of the apartment building where my grandmother lived approached my father to see if he was interested in buying the building. My father knew I had been saving money and offered the deal to me. I had strong motivation because I wanted to protect my grandmother from landlords who would raise her rent or kick her out in order to convert the apartments into condos. She had lived there for over 20 years and truly loved the place. While I certainly wasn't fully 'ready' to become a landlord, I 'FIRED', signing a purchase agreement and 'Corrected and Continued' in the months ahead. Believe me, I became a fast learner. It's still amazing to me how the Universe will provide opportunities to those who set out their Intentions and get into Action even without a clear idea of what the opportunity will look like. Learn and apply this principle and you will have set into motion one of the keys to achieving Financial Freedom. As a footnote to my story, my grandmother lived in my apartment building for 20 more years until she finally had to be moved to a nursing home in her mid-nineties. I am forever grateful and feel blessed that I had the opportunity to give her something that truly enriched her life.

Now, I'm not asking you to jump in and buy an apartment building, but I am asking you to get into *action*. Pull out your

'Vision Worksheet' and think of several actions that you could take in the next 7 days that would move you forward. It might be as simple as increasing your contribution to your company retirement plan, or developing a personal financial statement so that you know your 'starting point' for your Financial Freedom journey, or spending 30 minutes reading about how to get of debt. In the Get Rich On Purpose® book series, you can read about a very effective way to get out of debt fast in the *Debt Pyramid Reduction Strategy*, which is available on Kindle. Then implement (get into *action*) that strategy. You decide— big step, baby step—but get into *action.*

> *"Shallow men believe in luck; strong men believe in cause and effect."*
>
> —Thomas Watson

Opportunity Assignment

1. Adopt these two new mantras (you'll want to write these down and either carry them with you or post them

where they'll be a consistent reminder): READY, *FIRE,*

AIM! And CORRECT AND CONTINUE!

READY, FIRE, AIM!
CORRECT AND CONTINUE!

---

2. On your Vision Worksheet (Chapter 2), list several (minimum of 3) actions you can take over the next 7 days that will move you towards your Commitment to Financial Freedom.

3. Share your Action items with someone and ask them to hold you accountable for getting them done.

4. Remember, be willing to get in the game and take some action. Be willing to do what MOST people do not or will not do in order to achieve what most people will not accomplish. So, Take Some Action! If

you have done all of the Opportunity Assignments, you should feel the seeds of momentum beginning to sprout. Excellent! You know the routine—give yourself a pat on the back!

My thoughts from this chapter...

_____

_____

_____

_____

_____

_____

_____

Chapter 5

The Secret of Wisdom

When I was 22 years old and decided that I was going to become a millionaire, I had almost no knowledge of how to accomplish this monumental feat. But I did have the wisdom to recognize that I had to gain that knowledge *and* I was willing to commit myself to that task, *whatever it took*. Knowledge and wisdom are different concepts. Knowledge is the 'knowing' of something. Wisdom is the recognition of what you do know and can apply to a situation or problem. Wisdom is also understanding what you don't know, when to ask for help, and knowing what you need to learn in order to solve a problem. As it applies to Financial Freedom, you may know how to invest to earn 2–4 percent, but you may also recognize that you have not learned to earn 10, 20, 50, 100 percent or more. If your Financial Freedom goal requires returns that exceed your knowledge, then you must recognize that there is a gap between what you know versus what you must learn. Now you must choose the path(s) that will fill in this 'gap'. Understanding this is called *wisdom.*

You can read books, take courses or seminars, find a model or mentor or hire someone to help you. To create Financial Freedom for myself, I chose to study the strategies of others who had already become Self-Made Millionaires. I studied what they had done. I even hosted a TV show where I interviewed Self-Made Millionaires so I could learn more about the things they did that made them successful.

By studying Self-Made Millionaires, I began to learn how to make higher rates of return on my money. Now, when I talk about making rates of return that exceed 100 percent, people are naturally skeptical. By way of a recent example, I provided the money for a group who purchased and renovated a home for $52,000 and sold it 90 days later for $72,000 and we split the $20,000 profit. So what was the rate of return on my investment? On the surface, it appears to be approximately 20 percent. But that return was over 90 days. If I was able to duplicate that deal each of four quarters, I would have received $40,000 on a 12-month investment of $52,000, or about 80%. But instead of using cash, I used an interest-only bank line of credit, so my cash investment was only approximately $2,000 and resulted in returns of several hundred percent. I should note that my investment was secured by the deed to the property. I've done this type of transaction at least thirty times over the past three years.

Yes, you too can learn to earn higher rates of return on your money.

"Success leaves clues."

—Tony Robbins

An important disclaimer: I confess that not all of my investments have been this successful. In fact, in some cases,

I lost all my money. But my 'wins' have way outweighed my losses. One of my most important personal lessons learned is that success and failure are two sides of the same coin. In fact, virtually all success is built on the back of many failures.

Opportunity Assignment

Make a list of everything you can think of that you need to know to create Financial Freedom for yourself. Examples might include: where your finances are right now (a list of your assets, liabilities, and sources of income); your 'number'—how much money (or income) you need to reach Financial Freedom; your target date for accomplishing your goal along with the required rate of return; what you already know 'how' to invest in and what rate of return those investment vehicles earn versus what rate of return you need to earn and what types of investments have the potential to earn those rates of return; who or what (books, seminars, etc.) can help you fill the knowledge gap.

Once you have made as complete a list as possible, look back over your 'Action Plan' (the Secret of Decisive Action) and revise it according to your new 'wisdom'.

As you continue to seek wisdom, you will find it and it will continue to grow. Wisdom encompasses both the things that we find out work as well as the things that don't work. That's a beautiful thought because it means that everything that we learn, experience, hear, see or touch adds to our collective wisdom. Even your mistakes make you wiser!

My thoughts from this chapter…

_____

_____

_____

_____

_____

_____

_____

_____

Chapter 6

The Secret of Attitude

"Life is an attitude. You can either allow circumstances and events to disable you or empower you. The choice is yours. So, how is your life?"

—Stewart H. Welch, III

This is the one secret that can have the most impact on your life. I truly believe that if you'll embrace this one, it will improve the 'living' of living life in a very special way.

There has been an awful lot written about the importance of attitude and success. So much so that mentioning attitude becomes almost a turn-off—a conversation stopper. So let›s settle this once and for all. Does attitude really play a role in the success of Self-Made Millionaires? Well, I have certainly witnessed some Self-Made Millionaires that did not have a good attitude. But, you know what? I was NOT anxious to spend much time with them. So the answer is that you don't HAVE to have a good attitude to become Financially Free, but why would you choose NOT to do so?

"A bad attitude invariably defeats the Universal Law of Attraction."

—Stewart H. Welch, III

I'm sure you are familiar with the Law of Attraction. It states that 'Like Attracts Like'. In other words, whatever you put out into the Universe comes back to you in a similar form. Let me see if I can bring this into perfect focus for you. Would you rather spend time with someone who is upbeat, energetic and fun-loving, or someone whose focus is mostly negative—on what's wrong with the world or what's wrong in their life? I think I know your answer. Here's a follow up question. If you intend to accumulate the wealth needed to become Financially Free, where will all of that money come from? I can feel your hesitation. The answer is *other people*. If all of your money will come from other people, it makes sense to me to develop a persona that is attractive—i.e. a good attitude. So how can you go from 'good' (I assume your attitude is at least good) to perfect (or at least near perfect)?

You may be saying this sounds like a lot of work! For today's lesson, I'm going to share with you a simple formula that can instantly create the *perfect attitude* every day and change your life. How do I know this? Because it changed mine! It›s called *The Power of 3-Squared + 3*. If you are willing to do this exercise for one week, I believe it will change your life too.

Here's the Formula:

1. **List 3 blessings.** Before rising each day, take a moment to focus on 3 things for which you are grateful. What you focus on in your life will expand; therefore take some time each day to remember the things in your life you are grateful for. Easy examples might include

your spouse, children or other relationships; your health; or owning a nice home.

2. **List 3 daily actions.** Before starting your day, write down the 3 most important things you need to accomplish this day. At least one of those actions must be focused on one of your predetermined intentions (i.e. achieving Financial Freedom). Don't end your day until all 3 are done. Be clear about your Intentions, and then take Action. **The Universe rewards Action.** For example, you might have an action to increase your company retirement plan contribution; or to walk (exercise) for 45 minutes.

3. **Uplift 3 people.** Commit to encouraging at least 3 people in a very specific way each day. You'll know you've achieved it when you see their life 'light up' in their eyes. Recently, I told the lady behind the deli counter at the grocery store that she had a pretty smile (she did!) and you could see that the

compliment 'landed'. She was a little 'taken back' but I could tell the compliment made her day!

4. **Celebrate 3 successes.** At the end of your day, identify and celebrate three 'wins' (positive results) for your day. These don't have to be 'mountain-mover' successes. You could celebrate having gone to the gym that day like you promised yourself, or completing a company project, or consuming a healthy diet. Big or small, take a moment to acknowledge and celebrate.

Opportunity Assignment

Follow **The Power of 3-Squared + 3** exercises for 7 days. I believe it will change your entire outlook on life!

TIP

Maintaining a daily journal is a great way to record your successes and a great source of encouragement to you if you ever feel a bit down. I would like to encourage you to record your results for the next 7 days. If this 7 day experiment works for you, continue to use it. If you have an accountability partner, let them be the first recipient of your 'Uplift 3 People' exercise and watch their eyes light up!

My thoughts from this chapter...

_____

_____

_____

_____

_____

_____

_____

_____

Chapter 7

The Secret of Financial Focus

"It is easy to dodge our responsibilities but we cannot dodge the consequences of dodging our responsibilities."

—Sir Josiah Stamp

One of the primary reasons people fail to create financial success in their lives is because they choose, either consciously or unconsciously, *not* to focus their attention on financial matters. Oh sure, they do the minimum—pay their bills (sometimes late) and maybe contribute some money to their company retirement plan, but they don't do what is required to succeed. Maybe it's because they are not sure where to begin, or maybe there's another reason. But in the end, their minimal effort creates minimal results.

"I'm going to run a marathon!"

A good analogy is running a marathon. Let's assume that you have not been involved in physical fitness for the last couple of decades. You decide that you are going to run and complete a marathon. There's one this weekend in your hometown. Are you going to sign up to run it? If you did, do you think you are likely to complete it? I suspect the answer to both questions is not just 'No', but 'HELL NO!' To successfully complete a marathon, you're going to need to re-focus your attention on getting into shape. You will need to develop and execute a fitness plan of continuous improvement that will get you 'physically ready' to achieve your goal.

Becoming Financially Free is very similar. People who do become Financially Free focus their attention on the steps, tools and processes needed to get the job done. Just like running a marathon requires muscle development, becoming Financially Free requires 'financial mind muscle' development. This Secret of Financial Focus falls under the Universal Law of Attention which states, "What you put your Attention (Focus) on expands." If you focus, or put attention and spend time on eating healthy, you will become healthier; if you focus on physical fitness, you will become more fit; if you focus on your personal finances, your finances will improve, especially when you combine that focus with your *intention* to become Financially Free—.i.e. when the focus of your intention is a 'positive' outcome. Here's an important distinction. If your increased financial focus is 'negative'—as in "bills, bills, bills'—your negative focus will expand and you'll get more of what? BILLS! I hope you see this distinction because it's critical.

So how do you go from where you are to where you need to be related to the Secret of Financial Focus?

First, you need to create a new *mindset,* or *paradigm,* in the way you view money. Under this new paradigm, think of your personal finances as if it were a business, like a Fortune 500 company. You have *revenue* (your salary or other income sources), you have *expenses* (your monthly and non-periodic bills), and you'll need to manage the two so that there is money left over—known as your *profit*. Your profit is reinvested so that you *grow your company* (i.e. your *net worth*).

Second, a paradigm you'll want to adopt is, "**Every Dollar Matters,**" meaning that it's your responsibility to make sure that every dollar you own is *working hard* for you. No idle money!

Have you every driven by a construction site and seen one person digging while three others are leaning on their shovels watching? It drives me crazy! Well, I visualize my 'dollar bills' as workers and I want them all working to make me money. This view has helped me pay attention to my money and create a faster tract to financial success.

Finally, you'll need to establish a new habit. If you really want to see change happen quickly, commit to spending 30 minutes per day on your personal finances. If you're not sure where to start, here are some ideas:

- Start with education. Read *The Fundamentals of Wealth Creation* or another book from the Get Rich On Purpose® book series, or any other book on personal finance. Commit to reading a minimum of one book per month to improve your education.

- Read research on your current mutual funds held in your retirement plan or personal account. Visit **www. Morningstar.com**.

- Create a Personal Financial Statement so that you know where you stand financially today. If you have never done a Personal Financial Statement, you can find a Template at the end of this chapter. You can also find a download and print a copy of this template from the Resource Section at **www. GetRichOnPurpose.com.** You can find more information about creating your Personal Financial Statement in *The Fundamentals of Wealth Creation* from the Get Rich On Purpose® book series.

- Continue to work on the Actions you wrote down on your "Vision Worksheet" after reading the Secret of Decisive Action, completing what you have and adding new ones.

What I've just described is what Self-Made Millionaires do naturally. They pay a lot of attention to their money—and their money expands.

Opportunity Assignment

The most important first step you need to take to become successful and to create that new mindset of treating your finances like a business is to determine your current 'baseline'. "Where are you right now, financially speaking?" To do this, you must complete a Personal Financial Statement, sometimes referred to as a Statement of Net Worth. Once completed, you will want to update it at least annually. At the end of this chapter you will find a simple form for completing your Personal Financial Statement.

> *"The number one problem with today's generation and economy is the lack of financial literacy."*
>
> —Alan Greenspan

Yep. Becoming Financially Free does require some effort on your part. As John Rohn says, *"You can't pay someone to do your push-ups!"*

Once you've completed your Personal Financial Statement, pat yourself on the back! That's actually a bigger deal than you think. Be sure to save each one. I look back at my early Statements and I am amazed at the progress!

<u>Statement of Net Worth</u>
<u>aka Personal Financial Statement</u>

Personal Assets: Value:
Cash
Money market funds
Savings account
Real estate (estimated current market value)
Residence
Farm
Other
Investments
Individual stocks
Individual bonds
Mutual funds
401(k)
IRA's
Other retirement plans
Closely held business (estimated current market value)
Equity interest
Financial Assets Sub-total:

Personal Assets	
Automobile	
Jewelry	
Other	
Personal Assets Subtotal:	
Assets Total Value:	

Liabilities:	Amount:
Personal line of credit (short term)	
Home mortgage(s)	
Automobile loan(s)	
Other	
Total Liabilities:	
Net Worth (Total Assets Minus Total Liabilities):	

My thoughts from this chapter…

_____

_____

_____

_____

_____

_____

_____

_____

Chapter 8

The Secret of Leverage

"Give me a lever long enough and a fulcrum on which to place it, and I shall move the world."

—Archimedes

Do you want to accelerate the speed at which you achieve Financial Freedom? Then you must learn how to incorporate *leverage* into your Financial Freedom plan. *Leverage* is the secret that will set you free!

I've already told you my story of 'Deciding' ("The Secret of Decision") that I would become a millionaire by age

40. Well, here's the rest of the story. Initially, I was in insurance sales, which paid the bills and supported my lifestyle, but my 'millionaire plan' was to buy one piece of real estate per year. I hatched this idea because I noticed that that's what a lot of Self-Made Millionaires did and I was simply modeling their behavior. My assumption was that in 15 years, I'd own 15 pieces of real estate and was bound to be a millionaire, right?

Well, actually that *did* work. In continuing my study of Self-Made Millionaires, I also noticed that for many, the key to their success was owning a business. So in 1984, I set my Intention on building a million-dollar business. At the time, my definition (Vision) of a million-dollar business was a business that I could *sell* for a million dollars if I chose to do so. So I developed a **Written Plan of Action** for something that was very rare at that time—a *fee-only* investment management and financial advisory firm. The vast majority of people in the financial advice business at that time sold products and lived off commissions. I wanted to build a financial advice business model based on the typical accounting practice model. I worked very hard, learned from my mistakes (remember your mantra 'Correct and Continue'!) and ended up building two fee-only financial advisory companies which together are worth several million dollars.

So here I was worth a pile of money *on paper.* Wow, I was proud of myself! Then it dawned on me—I was working 60 to 80 hours or more every week—including, often, weekends. I also noticed I was feeling a bit of burn-out and wasn't feeling as happy as I thought I should. There had to be something better. Then it dawned on me that true Financial Freedom was something else. Financial Freedom, it seems, is achieved only when actually going to work is a *choice*! It certainly wasn't a choice for me! Maybe I could take a few days off here and there, but if I wasn't there for long, the wheels would begin to come off the wagon. I suspect some of you can relate to this. I made a 'decision' right then to go back and work 'ON' my business so that I didn't have to work 'IN' my business unless I chose to. I activated **The Secret of Decisive**

Action and hired a COO (chief operations officer), set up a management team with outlined responsibilities, and then left for 6 months to see how it would work! I used the time to write a book, *The Complete Idiot's Guide to Getting Rich*— and I stayed close enough to 'monitor' how the business was doing. When I returned, I realized it was running better without me! Scary thought! But I realized I was now free to focus my time on things I loved doing and was passionate about (examples include reaching out to thousands of people with books like this!). In doing so, I went from 'not so happy' to really happy almost overnight. It's surprising how happy you are when you spend your time doing things you are truly passionate about.

So how does my story relate to the **Secret of Leverage** and how do you apply the secret in your own life? The moral of my story is this: There are lots of Self-Made Millionaires who are NOT Financially Free. *The key to Financial Freedom is leverage through creating passive income streams.* How much passive income? Enough to pay for your desired lifestyle! Make sense? Well, how are YOU going to do this?

First, change your *mindset* about how you'll create Financial Freedom for yourself. Starting now, think of creating building blocks of passive income. Then apply the **Secret of Decisive Action** and create your first, or second, or next passive income 'building block'. In other words, *get into action*! For the moment, I don't care where you start. It could be a savings account that's producing $1 per month of *continuous passive income*. The important thing is to set it up and segregate it from everything else. This money is now 'untouchable' and will never be used except as part of your Financial Freedom plan. Once it's set up, you'll 'educate' yourself on how to increase the passive income through smarter investing.

You can use the Secret of Leverage to create passive income which can be created in many forms but the effect is to 'magnify' your results. I discuss this extensively in *The Fundamentals of Wealth Creation*, in the Get Rich On Purpose®

book series,   but here's the *Reader's Digest* version on using *the secret of leverage* to create passive income:

Leverage through compounding interest.

Let's begin with a discussion of the most basic forms of leverage. Albert Einstein said that compound interest is the 8th wonder of the world; I know you may know something about compound interest, but I'd like to show it to you in a little different way. Let's assume that you're investing $833 dollars a month, or about $10,000 a year. Most people think about it like this: they know their money is growing but they assume it's growing more in a straight line, called a 'linear' progression. The reality is that because you are earning interest on not only the amount of money you invested but you're also earning interest on the interest. From your investment you have what's called compound growth, or 'geometric' progression. As you continue to invest that money, compounding on itself, it begins to grow in a more rapid way and you move into what I call "the power curve."

That's when something very interesting begins to happen. Let's assume that with that $10,000 dollar annual investment you're earning 10 percent. In approximately year 8 you move to what I call '1 to 1'. That means that you're contributing $10,000 dollars, but the amount of money and the interest that you're earning on that is also contributing $10,000 dollars. It took us 8 years to get there. Because we moved into that power curve it only takes us 4 more years to get to what I call '2 to 1'. That's where you're contributing $10,000 dollars, but your investment account (i.e. the 'pot') is now producing $20,000 dollars a year in interest. It only takes 3 more years to get to '3 to 1', and 2 more years to get to '4 to 1'. At this point the pot is earning $40,000 dollars a year in interest while you continue to contribute $10,000 dollars. Now what's really important about the program is that in the early stage the most important thing is the 'consistency of investing'. This is literally putting the money in month-in and month-out. However once you begin to move into the power curve what becomes most important is the 'rate of return'.

STEWART H WELCH III

What I haven't told you is that I am also a mind reader and I know what you're thinking. You're thinking you can't get 10 percent, so this is not a very good example. The reality is that you CAN get 10 percent, and if you're not getting 10 percent on your investments, you just need to *learn* how to earn a higher rate of return.

As an example, I have a promissory note that's currently paying me 14%. Once you learn to earn at higher rate of return, compound interest can be a very effective tool on your path of wealth accumulation. Can the 'leverage effect' of compounding really make a difference even with small amounts of money? Read the story of Oseola McCarty...

Oseola McCarty was born in 1908 in Mississippi. At the age of 6, her aunt got sick, and Oseola quit school to take care of her and later became a washerwoman, cleaning clothes for local families. Her mother had taught her the importance of saving, so she opened a savings account at the local bank and consistently made deposits from her meager earnings. She continued to work and save until arthritis prevented her from doing so at age 86. She died of cancer at age 91. Before she died, she had a will drawn where she left a $150,000 endowment to the University of Southern Mississippi to fund scholarships for disadvantaged students. Plus, there was another $100,000 that she left to family! Here's a lady who never earned more than poverty-level wages who, through consistent saving and compound interest, left a lasting legacy.

Leverage through stocks.

Stocks present a unique form of leverage. You may not know how to run a Fortune 500 company, but you can invest in someone who does. When you buy stocks in a public corporation, what you're really doing is investing in the management team. And while we all know that corporate CEO's and upper management can make large salaries, their true wealth comes from something called stock options. They're given an opportunity to buy lots of shares in the future at the current stock price or a predetermined stock price. So their objective is to grow the value of the company and therefore grow the stock price. As they do that, they become very, very rich. The form of leverage to you is what I call intellectual leverage. You're investing in their particular skill set and you're able to 'ride their coattails' to their success and your success as well—assuming they are successful. For example, if Oseola, in our story above, had consistently invested in the stock market, it's estimated that her $250,000 estate would have been nearly $1,000,000! Historically, the stock market has earned 8–10 percent over long periods of time. If you plan to use stocks as part of your 'building blocks' of Passive Income, you'll want to consider the Rising Dividend Stock Strategy as described in *Becoming a Smart Investor,* in the Get Rich On Purpose® book series.

Leverage through tax planning.

Whether you live in the United States of America or another country, you will have tax policy that allows you to leverage your money and grow your wealth faster. Here in America, the government wants to promote saving for your retirement, so they give incentives to do so. Many companies offer pre-tax payroll deduction plans into a company retirement plan. These same companies often also offer incentives to save by 'matching' a portion of your contributions. Outside of company retirement plans are a variety of tax deductible retirement plans including IRA, SEP (for self-employed persons), and Roth IRA tax-deferred plans (Roth's are not tax deductible). Investing before the government scrapes off 30–40 percent in taxes can really ramp up your wealth. Combine tax leverage with Passive Income Building Blocks whose interest, dividends, etc. grow without being taxed, and you can achieve amazing results.

Pay attention, please!

Too often, people don't pay attention to the importance of tax leverage. For example, I met with a prospective client, and after reviewing his financial information, I asked him why he wasn't contributing to his company 401k plan, particularly since the company matched his contributions $1 for $1 up to 6 percent of pay. His response was, "I can't afford to." However, he was 'investing' in a cash value life insurance policy and mutual funds on a monthly basis. I pointed out to him how his investment in his company's 401k yielded a guaranteed 100 percent rate of return in the first year of each contribution because of the match. He needed the life insurance, but we were able to do some 'rearranging,' including taking advantage of the new tax deduction he received for his 401k contribution so that he could maintain adequate life insurance and continue investing a portion of his income in personal mutual funds while capturing the full matching contribution from his employer. Here's a quick comparative example that shows the power of investing $10,000 annually through a company 401k plan matched dollar-for-dollar versus taking the after-tax proceeds and investing in the exact same mutual fund personally. Assuming thirty-five years and earning 8 percent, the 401k plan would have about $4 million while the after-tax personal investment plan (25 percent tax rate assumed) would have about $1.5 million. It's true that I've ignored the fact that as funds are withdrawn from the 401k plan, they will be taxed, but I also ignored ongoing taxes on earnings (interest, dividends, and realized capital gains) from the personal investment program. The magnitude of the difference is apparent. Use of leverage in the form of a tax deduction and years of tax deferred growth is an excellent wealth building strategy.

So far, we've talked about two of the most basic forms of leverage. In my research, there have been lots of people who have become millionaires using either or both of those methods. However they tend to take a long time: 20 years, 30 years, 40 years or more. If you want to move into the highest forms of leverage, here's where we see the most millionaires being made. It is in two primary categories. The first one is leverage through investment real estate and the second is leverage through business ownership.

Leverage through real estate.

Investment Real Estate uses a particular form of leverage called *financial leverage*. Financial Leverage looks something like this; let's assume that you have the opportunity to buy a duplex apartment for $100,000 dollars. You could pay $100,000 cash. After 12 months, your net income (after expenses) would be $10,000 dollars. What is your rate of return? It's 10 percent. You put down $100,000 and you got $10,000 of net income. What if, instead of paying $100,000 in cash, you invest $20,000 in cash and then go over to the bank and borrow $80,000? At the end of 12 months, your net income is $7,000 (net is lower due to interest payments). Now what is your rate of return? Your rate of return moved up to 35 percent because you put down $20,000 dollars in cash and you managed to still have $7,000 dollars in net revenue. What if you took your remaining $80,000 and purchased four more apartment complexes under the same formula? Instead of receiving $10,000 of cash flow annually, you'd be receiving $35,000. That's financial leverage, and lots of people have become millionaires investing in real estate. The most famous example would be Donald Trump.

Even better, the government will allow you to use Tax Leverage to compound your Financial Leverage in Real Estate. The government will allow you to deduct the interest! To make things even better, the government allows you to use tax leverage by allowing you to 'depreciate' your property! The government assumes that all of your 'brick & mortar' is going down in value even if it is going up! If you want to achieve Financial Freedom very fast, real estate is still one of your best choices. Yep, if you are going to use this strategy, you're going to have to 'learn' how to invest in real estate, but this is something that you absolutely can do!

Leverage through business ownership.

While starting up or buying a business may be the most challenging paths to Financial Freedom, it is also the one most Self-Made Millionaires have taken. In fact, entrepreneurs account for about 75% of Self-Made Millionaires. Here leverage can come in many forms—**financial leverage** as the business owner borrows money to grow the business, and **tax leverage** as hundreds of deductions are available to business owners that are not available to ordinary citizens. Perhaps the most important leverage is people leverage. Bringing together the right team of people can exponentially accelerate your results.

To use people leverage, surround yourself with people—a team. It could be people in the form of employees, or people in the form of mentors, coaches, or professionals. The concept is to be able to leverage your skill set and your time. As a personal example, in my companies, I have lots of talented people who are working with me. Some of them have expertise in areas I have no experience or talent; others are doing things that I am not very passionate about doing. What this allows me to do is not only focus on the things I like to do, but it allows me to focus on the things I do best. Being able to surround myself with this team, I am able to create companies that create millions of dollars in revenue rather than tens of thousands of dollars in revenue.

You can learn more about creating wealth by starting your own business in *Building Wealth With Your Own Business*, available in the Get Rich On Purpose® book series.

From the basement to the richest man on Earth

A famous example of using people leverage is Bill Gates. He dropped out of college and started his computer business in the basement of his parents' home. He started with one employee, and that employee was Bill Gates. He had a dream, and that dream was to put desktop computing in every home on the planet. To do that, Bill was astute enough to put together a team of people who were the most talented, most sophisticated players in the space of software development. The rest is history. He built one of the biggest software companies in the world and became one of the richest men in the world.

So how are you going to use **The Secret of Leverage** in your own plan to achieve Financial Freedom? I don't know. You tell me.

Opportunity Assignment

Review your Commitment form and reconsider your current strategy for achieving Financial Freedom. Would you be willing to 'learn' how to invest in the stock market; invest in real estate; or build a successful business in order to accelerate your success? Make a list of the Critical Success Factors—the knowledge, the people, the team, and the tools that must come together for you to be successful in the path you've chosen. Remember, the Universe connects to all things, and all of the answers to all of your questions are out there. You just need to know where to go or whom to ask.

1. Set up one passive income structure as part of your Financial Freedom plan.

2. Share the concept of 'Building Blocks of Passive Income' with someone along with the building block you just created.

<u>Resources</u>: For in-depth reading on this topic, consider these books from the Get Rich On Purpose® book series:

Becoming A Smart Investor

Building Wealth With Your Own Business

My wife likes to say, "Bloom where you are planted." Start from wherever you are and build your Financial Freedom from there—one step at a time, one day at a time.

> *None of us can change our yesterdays,*
> *but all of us can change our tomorrows.*
>
> —Colin Powell

Wow! Once you've set up a Passive Income Investment, you're on your way! Give yourself a double pat on the back!

My thoughts from this chapter…

_____

_____

_____

_____

_____

_____

_____

Chapter 9

The Secret of Team

*"I figured out that life in general is a team effort;
it's a team game."*

—Joe Namath

This naturally leads me to the 9th secret—The Secret of *team*. Rarely have I met a Self-Made Millionaire who got there without a lot help. In fact, built into most Self-Made Millionaires' DNA is the intuitive knowledge that they'll need to develop a Team, seek out Mentors, and Model others who have gone where they intend to go.

There are several ways to use the Secret of Team to increase your power to achieve, receive and retain Wealth and Financial Freedom. One of the most dangerous pitfalls is trying to be the 'lone ranger' or the trap of trying to 'DIY' (Do It Yourself). Self-Made Millionaires use some or all of the following strategies in order to surround themselves with a team of people who help them along their path to success.

Surround yourself with successful people.

Spend time with other successful people; people who have similar goals and values to the ones they have; and those who have already achieved what they want to achieve. This can be done through networking in a number of ways.

Know your strengths and weaknesses.

Identify your strengths and weaknesses, and 'hire out' or 'partner' with those who are strong in areas where you do not have knowledge or expertise, or possibly with those who enjoy doing things that you do not enjoy.

Seek help from others.

Be open to and willing to benefit from the accumulated experience and knowledge of others. Self-Made Millionaires identify the areas of expertise where they need help and are willing to seek out the experts to support them. Some people feel they cannot afford to pay for the top experts in their field. Self-Made Millionaires know intuitively that this is among the best investments they can make.

Think win-win.

Think 'win-win' rather than being fearful of competition or trying to always make certain you get the biggest piece of the pie.

Have an open mind.

Be open to considering new ideas, and are willing to listen to others who have knowledge, insight and perhaps a new way of looking at things. This is not to say you want to be told what to do or want someone else to solve your problems. Gather as much quality information and knowledge as you can from your team quickly, and take it into consideration when you are making decisions.

How do you begin to use the Secret of Team? One of the best starting places is to find a Mentor—someone who will take you by the hand and lead you through the wilderness to the land of your dreams. Without a guide, most people will get hopelessly lost somewhere along the way and will settle for retracing their steps only to arrive back where they started—a place of familiarity—but also a place of self-disappointment.

Opportunity Assignment

Seek out a Mentor who will agree to guide you to your intended destination. You have lots of choices. Perhaps you know a Self-Made Millionaire personally who would be happy to mentor you.

Self-Made Millionaire Robert G. Allen said it well:

"Study someone who's great and you'll find that they apprenticed to a master, or several masters. Therefore, if you want to achieve greatness, renown and superlative success, you must apprentice a master."

My thoughts from this chapter…

_____

_____

_____

_____

_____

_____

_____

_____

Chapter 10

The Secret of Giving Back

"In helping others, we shall help ourselves, for whatever good we give out completes the circle and comes back to us."

—Flora Edwards

One of the main characteristics of virtually all Self-Made Millionaires is that they find a way to give back to the community in a way that truly changes lives for the better. This 'giving back' can be as simple and straightforward as giving money or time to charities, acting as a mentor, or advocating for a cause through public speaking or writing. Think of the word we use for money: currency. The word *currency* comes from the Latin word meaning "to run or flow." Money and wealth are not meant to be hoarded, but to flow like a river. Money is energy, life energy. Anything which is of value, including money, multiplies when it is given. This is one of the laws of nature and of the Universe.

There are no rules that require that this service to the community be free. In fact, it's often the case that a for-profit outreach strategy is able to significantly magnify the number of people touched and impacted. Tony Robbins is a great example. Through his various courses, he has been able to positively change the lives of hundreds of thousands of people.

The two most important days in your life are the day you are born and the day you find out why.

—Mark Twain

I believe that we each entered this world for a specific purpose, with certain talents that are our duty to share. To withhold our talents for fear of rejection or fear of failure is to cheat the Universe of what the Universe both expects of you and deserves from you.

On a personal level, I realized that I have the ability to look at people's finances and know what they need to do to become Financially Free. What if, in my remaining time on this planet, I could help one million families experience the exhilaration of being Financially Free? Now that would be a life worth living!

What are your talents, and how could you best share them with the world around you? If you had to come up with a strategy for sharing your talents with as many people as possible as quickly as possible, what would that strategy look like? When you combine your own unique talents with service to others, you can expect to experience abundance.

Opportunity Assignment

Write a Personal Mission Statement that incorporates your God-given talents. Include a brief (or detailed) Action Plan and a 'First Step.' What action could you take this week that would start you on the path of your mission? Take a few minutes and go through this exercise. You might just surprise yourself and set in motion your one true destiny!

Everyone has a purpose in life…a unique gift or special talent to give to others. And when we blend this talent with service to others, we experience the ecstasy and exultation of our own spirit, which is the ultimate goal of all goals.

—Deepak Chopra

My thoughts from this chapter...

_____

_____

_____

_____

_____

_____

_____

The Final Chapter (or is it?)

The Secret to Success:
The Magic Formula

We have covered the 10 secrets of how Self-Made Millionaires THINK. Remember, everyone possesses at least some of the secrets, but it's the possession of all ten that separate those who just get by versus those who enjoy the Financial Freedom life. It's important to understand all ten secrets and incorporate them into the fiber of your life. There may also be a way to incorporate them into a condensed version of the 10 secrets, a shortcut to success. What if there was a 'Magic Formula' that would guarantee you could become, have or achieve anything you truly desired? Think for a moment. If you possessed such a magic formula, what would you choose to accomplish? In the financial arena, what would you buy? Where would you live? What would your home be like? Would you travel, and to where? What kind of relationships would you have? Would you learn to speak multiple foreign languages? Would you author a best-selling book? What would your career look like? What would be your contribution to humanity?

Well, there is a magic formula for achieving anything you truly want in life…and here it is:

$$V + A = D$$

'V' stands for Vision. Most people 'settle' for a day-to-day existence, but there is a much bigger world out there that is full of adventure, excitement and fulfillment for those who dare to break out of their comfort zone, stretch themselves and seek to achieve their true potential. In order to achieve extraordinary results in your life, you must have a clear vision of what you truly desire. The clearer the vision, the easier and faster it is to accomplish.

On January 9, 1970, a struggling young actor wrote himself a letter stating that "by 1980, I will be the best known Oriental movie star in the United States and will secure $10 million dollars. In return, I'll give the very best acting I can possibly give every single time I am in front of the camera." In 1973, Bruce Lee starred in *Enter the Dragon* and became an instant martial arts legend and international superstar. His untimely death robbed him of the full realization of the achievement of his vision, but martial artists around the world benefited as he set a new standard for martial arts excellence.

Several elements have proven vital to this 'Vision' stage of self-manifestation:

- **Write it down.** Visualization is a powerful tool. When you take your vision from your mind's eye and convert it to writing, something truly magical happens. Research suggests that the mere act of writing a goal increases the likelihood of accomplishing it by 200 percent. That's because the process of written articulation creates a connection with your brain, and in turn, the Universe. As I've already stated, my personal belief is that God created the Universe and everything in it... so everything and every person is connected. All of the answers to all of your questions are available if you just know where to look or whom to ask. Once you write out your vision, your brain then sets about the business of solving the problem that exists between where you are right now and your intention (vision). It will work both on a conscious and subconscious level constantly sorting through possibilities and seeking solutions to the puzzle you have created. This process of searching and sorting will open doors you never expected and give you an extra-sensory awareness related to your vision. Expect miracles to happen.

3. **Clarity of Vision.** As I've already stated, the clearer your vision, the easier it is to accomplish because you are excited and focused, and you have engaged the Universe in your cause. Instead of writing, "I want a winter vacation home," write "I want a 5,000 square foot home facing east on the shore of Maui by noon the day before Thanksgiving 2017." Continue to describe what your dream home looks like in as much detail as possible. Be specific about the type of construction, interior furnishings, infinity swimming pool, and all glass across the ocean-facing side of your home. Clarity includes making certain that your goal, this vision, is measurable by both you and someone else and typically answers two questions: How much (or what)?/ and By when? To help 'see' the vision, some people use 'vision boards', which are cut-outs of magazine photos that depict their goals or virtual vision boards using the Internet. For example, if you'd like to own a yacht, find a picture of the yacht of your dreams and post

it where you'll see it every day as a reminder of your goal. When NASA began the planning and work for sending a man to the moon, they painted a moon, floor to ceiling, in the construction area to keep them perfectly focused on their vision. There are web sites that allow you to create a virtual vision board. Google 'Vision Boards'. Professional speaker and author John Assaraf cut out a magazine photo of his 'dream' home in 1995 and put it up on his Vision Board, then a few months later forgot about it. Five years later, as he was opening boxes from the move to his new 7,000 square foot residence, he pulled out and dusted off his Vision Board and began to weep as he realized that he was now living in the exact home he had envisioned. Not a similar home, but the exact one he had cut out! The Universe works in mysterious ways once you get in alignment.

- **Dream Big Dreams.** When I originally began creating a vision for what I wanted to accomplish in my life, much of what I sought seemed like the equivalent of climbing Mt. Everest: insurmountable. My vision included becoming a published author, a millionaire, a guest expert on national television such as CNN, and building a multimillion dollar company. When I reflect back on these goals, I actually feel a twinge of embarrassment that I didn't dream 'bigger'. This is normal for most people. Now I realize that what we can accomplish is only limited by our ability to dream big dreams. Many of us will have to learn to exercise our dream 'muscle' as we achieve, learn and grow emotionally. As one vision becomes reality, it signals the timing for creating a bigger and more compelling vision. One helpful tool you can use is what I call the Dream Big Dreams list. The idea is to make a list of 101 accomplishments or lifetime milestones you would achieve if there were no barriers to your

STEWART H WELCH III

success: unlimited financial resources, intelligence, and physical capability.

John Goddard (**www.JohnGoddard.info**) did this at age 15 when he developed his Life List of 127 goals. He had some big goals including climbing Mt. Kilimanjaro, Mt. Rainier, and Mt. Everest; exploring the Amazon River; learning to fly a plane; and flying in a blimp, balloon, and glider. This list from a 15-year-old boy turned into a lifetime of adventure and learning where only 15 of the original 127 goals remain. The purpose of the Dream Big Dreams list is to, well, dream. Get your creative juices flowing and write down everything you could imagine would excite you and create a life of fulfillment and adventure. From there, you can narrow your focus to a few key areas that create the most 'charge' for you. Typically one or a small number of items will bubble up in the form of 'burning desire'. You'll know burning desire because when you are working on them, it's not like work at

114

all. It's the feeling of passion. At this point, you'll write a vision statement in as much detail as possible. Then you can begin to develop an Action Plan for turning your vision into reality.

'A' stands for Action. The Universe rewards action; or as comedian/actor Jonathan Winters says, "If your ship doesn't come in, swim out to meet it!" Once you have a clear written vision of what you intend to achieve, you'll want to develop an Action Plan to help you get there as quickly as possible. In most cases you will not know all of the steps necessary to achieve your vision, but invariably you'll know the first few steps. If not, ask someone who has gone before you. You'll find most people are more than willing to help fellow travelers. Be satisfied to take the action steps that you are aware of and trust that the Universe will illuminate your path as you continue to travel. It's like driving a car at 60 miles per hour down a two-lane country road in the middle of the night. Your headlights only allow you to see maybe 70 yards ahead of you. You have no idea what might be ahead in the darkness. Yet you continue to press forward, trusting that your path will continue to illuminate as you continue to drive at 60 miles per hour.

My First TV Appearance

Speaking of 'trusting the Universe,' I remember envisioning becoming a financial 'expert' on TV and writing down my vision, not having any idea how I would make this happen. One day, a local television station announced they were starting a morning show. Because I had *written down* the goal (vision), I 'forced' myself to call the station and ask if I could meet with the hosts about me becoming their financial expert. Their response was that they already had a financial expert but I persevered and they agreed (reluctantly I believe) to visit with me. Of course I went in prepared with sample topics and questions they could use…I had the whole thing laid out for them 'nice and easy'. They agreed to give me an opportunity share the expert spot, alternating weeks with the current expert. I continued to work hard to make their life very easy, and soon I was the sole financial expert for the show. I've now appeared as the financial expert on the top rated TV program for more than twenty years! I've also appeared on CNN, CNBC and Fox News in New York.

There is a saying that goes, "A journey of a thousand miles begins with a single step." The journey to the realization of your vision will be made of many steps, some small, and some giant leaps. The key to maximum speed is to develop an attitude of 'disciplined action'—creating a process whereby you are consistently moving forward until you are at your destination. Start by brainstorming, on paper, a list of Critical Success Factors (CSF) with a timetable. What are the key things that 'must happen' in order for you to succeed? What is your target completion date? Under each CSF, list all the Supporting Actions (SA) that will move you closer to your CSF. This will be a 'work in progress' as you will continually add to your action list as you check off completed actions. Then, every evening, make a list of 1-3 SAs to complete the next day and commit to getting them done before your day is finished. When you're done with one SA, ask, "What's next?" and add to your list. Keep track of your progress and be sure to celebrate your successes…even the small ones.

Avoid 'paralysis by analysis' and adopt the mantra, "Ready, FIRE, Aim." Too many people get bogged down in analyzing the problem or waiting for the perfect time to execute their strategy. All successful people are highly action oriented. They'll spend some time brainstorming the Critical Success Factors and the companion Supporting Actions, but then they'll jump in the game knowing they'll need to 'correct course' as they continue on their journey. A great analogy for 'correct and continue' is flying a plane. If after taking off you simply chose a correct course heading, say due north, and held that position, you would miss your destination. That's because you would be required to make numerous 'course corrections' for a variety of unpredictable reasons, including wind speed, wind direction and barometric pressure. For you, this means get in the game as quickly as possible and expect to make numerous course corrections along the way as you'll 'learn' (make mistakes) your way to success.

Somewhere along your journey, you're likely to come face-to-face with the proverbial 'brick wall' and wonder whether it's time to give up on your vision. Consider this a test of your tenacity and commit to going over, around or through the wall, whatever it takes. You can get leverage on your success journey by having an accountability/support partner. This can either be one person or, even better, a small group of people (a mastermind group). The idea is to communicate your vision and your group agrees to support you and hold you accountable for the actions and timetables you've committed to. This is done through periodic contact (weekly, monthly, via phone, email, etc.).

This leads to my final thoughts on the importance of disciplined action. Never underestimate the importance of pure unadulterated perseverance. Tell yourself (out loud as a daily exercise), "I can achieve anything!" and "I will never give up!" For it is in perseverance that success lies. A great example of perseverance comes from Jack Canfield and Mark Victor Hanson. Unknown at the time, they had co-authored their first book called *Chicken Soup for the Soul,* which was a compilation of heartwarming stories. The problem was that no publisher thought much of their idea. They got turned down not once, not a dozen times, but 144 times before they finally found a publisher who believed in their dream. How many of us would have given up after one, two, or a dozen rejections? Jack and Mark persevered and they became two of the most prolific and successful authors in America, selling well over 100 million copies of their books. Never, ever give up on your dreams!

'D' is for Destiny. Each of us is unique and perfect in our own way and has been placed on this planet for a reason. Rather than drifting through 75 to 100 years allowing life to happen to you, wouldn't it be better to seek to discover your true purpose and then live out your life striving to achieve your maximum potential? By developing a clear vision for your life, one that is compelling, exciting, fulfilling and improves our universal community, and then executing a disciplined Action Plan, you can take control of your own destiny. We are able to create the life *we* choose—and not just in the area of finances, but in every area of our lives.

Do not be fooled by the simplicity of The Magic Formula for Success. Too often people decide that an answer is so 'simple' that it couldn't possibly work, so they discard it in search for something more complex. 'Simple' is very different from 'easy'. If you choose to do nothing, then you must settle for being a passenger on the bus of life with destination unknown. However, if you choose to take control, then you become the *driver*. You get to decide whether you drive a Ford or a Ferrari. You can make life as exciting as you choose. You see, the choice has always been and will always be *your* choice. Choose your destiny wisely!

The Big Question...

If you're reading this, you've finished the book, so congratulations! I hope you learned some pearls of wisdom that will change your life. There is one final, big question to ask. **Did you complete the exercises outlined in the**

Opportunity Assignments? Yes or no? Are you one of those people who likes to read the book first with the intention of going back and completing the exercises? Good intentions don't equal results. It's not enough to know what to do. You actually have to do it! By following the exercises in this book, you will create a living, breathing financial plan that will create the destiny of your dreams. I wish you Godspeed.

Appendix A

Turning Dreams into Reality

Few of us take the time to stop and take stock of our lives, but if you take a moment to reflect, you will find that you, in fact, accomplished quite a lot in the past year. But did you achieve your full potential? It's likely that your full potential is much greater than even you recognize. I'm reminded of the story of the dog whose owner always kept him in the backyard on a 25-foot chain. The owner fed and cared for him and sometimes even played with him. But the dog was always chained. After a time, the owner unbuckled the chain, but the dog never ventured beyond the 25-foot perimeter, now shackled by an artificial chain and collar. What's holding you back from achieving your full potential? Have you created your own artificial chain and collar? For each of us, our destiny is to have an extraordinary life. Yet it is up to us to claim it. I challenge you to commit to break the chains that are keeping you from achieving your true potential.

Achieving extraordinary results rarely happens by accident. First you have to decide exactly what it is you want, then believe that it is possible, develop a plan of action, and finally commit 100 percent to getting the results you intended. It's also important to acknowledge that success is rarely a sprint, but rather a marathon. In my experience, many people are good 'starters' but few are good 'finishers'. Use the following process to help you turn your biggest dreams into reality:

Develop your dream list. Start with a blank paper and write down everything you would do, own, buy, and accomplish if there were absolutely no barriers to your success. List everything you can imagine. This is where you want to think big and have some fun. Create a 'Vision' of your future. What would you be willing to totally commit to accomplishing?

From your dream list, choose one or two for which you feel the strongest passion and write them down on a separate piece of paper. The greater the detail, the better. Develop an Action Plan. Between where you are now and the achievement of your vision, you'll find a number of 'Critical Success Factors (CSF)'. These are the critical things that you must do to create success. List as many as you can think of along with supporting 'actions'. Include 'target timelines' for each CSF.

Commit 100 percent! Commitment is evidenced by daily focus. I believe that whatever you constantly focus on will come to pass. It is this constant focus that is the engine for achieving greatness. Each day you should include a minimum of three 'action activities' that move you closer to the realization of your vision. You can have the life of your dreams if you'll accept the responsibility for making your dreams a reality.

About the Author

Stewart H. Welch, III

Stewart is the creator and visionary for Get Rich on Purpose®. His mission is to provide resources for financial education and entrepreneurial development to individuals seeking to create sustainable financial freedom. His goal is to help those who need help and have a burning desire to become financially self-reliant.

Stewart formed his first fee-only financial advisory firm in 1984—a time when fee-only firms were very rare. He is the founder of two fee-only advisory firms: The Welch Group, LLC and Fee-Only Planning Professionals, LLC. Together these firms have helped hundreds of families across America.

Money, Worth, Mutual Funds magazine and *Medical Economics* have named Stewart as one of the top financial advisors in the United States. The Welch Group, LLC, has also been named one the 150 top financial advisory firms in America by *Bloomberg Wealth Manager* magazine.

Stewart regularly appears on TV and radio shows, including a weekly guest appearance on Fox TV. Nationally, he has appeared on CNBC, CNN and Fox News. His comments and advice have appeared in *The Wall Street Journal, Money, Kiplinger's Personal Finance, Smart Money, The New York Times* and *Forbes.* He is a financial columnist for AL.com, Alabama's largest digital/print news media, and has authored or co-authored: *The Complete Idiot's Guide To Getting Rich, J.K. Lasser's New Rules for Estate and Tax Planning, J.K. Lasser's Estate Planning for Baby Boomers and Retirees, 10 Minute Guide to Personal Finances for Newlyweds;* as well as his *Get Rich on Purpose®* series.

His firm, The Welch Group, LLC, **www.WelchGroup.com**, provides fee-only investment management and financial advisory services to affluent families throughout the United